HISTORY'S GREATEST R

ALEXANDER HAMILTON Vs. AARON BURR

DUEL TO THE DEATH

Ellis Roxburgh

Gareth Stevens
PUBLISHING

Please visit our website, **www.garethstevens.com**. For a free color catalog of all our high-quality books, call toll-free 1-800-542-2595 or fax 1-877-542-2596.

Library of Congress Cataloging-in-Publication Data
Roxburgh, Ellis.
 Alexander Hamilton vs. Aaron Burr : duel to the death / Ellis Roxburgh.
    pages cm. — (History's great rivals)
 Includes index.
 ISBN 978-1-4824-2214-6 (pbk.)
 ISBN 978-1-4824-2215-3 (6 pack)
 ISBN 978-1-4824-2213-9 (library binding)
 1. Burr-Hamilton Duel, Weehawken, N.J., 1804—Juvenile literature.
 2. Hamilton, Alexander, 1757-1804—Juvenile literature.
 3. Burr, Aaron, 1756-1836—Juvenile literature. I. Title.
 E302.6.H2R69 2015
 973.4'6092—dc23

                        2014031129

Published in 2015 by
Gareth Stevens Publishing
111 East 14th Street, Suite 349
New York, NY 10003

© 2015 Brown Bear Books Ltd

For Brown Bear Books Ltd:
Editorial Director: Lindsey Lowe
Managing Editor: Tim Cooke
Children's Publisher: Anne O'Daly
Design Manager: Keith Davis
Designer: Lynne Lennon
Picture Manager: Sophie Mortimer

Picture Credits
Front Cover: Robert Hunt Library: left; National Portrait Gallery right; Shutterstock: background. Art Archive: Museum of the City of New York 13; Library of Congress: 7, 8, 12, 26, 27, 29, 32, 34, 37; Museum of the City of New York: 24; National Portrait Gallery: ifcl, 4, 10, 42; New York Historical Society: 15, 28, 31, 33; Robert Hunt Library: ifcr, 5, 11, 14, 16, 17, 19, 22, 23, 30, 36, 43; Shutterstock: 4/5, 9, 40, 41, 42/43; TopFoto: Granger Collection 38, 39; U.S. Architect of the Capitol: 6, 45; U.S. National Archives: 20, 21; Whitehouse Historical Association: 25. Artistic Effects Shutterstock

Brown Bear Books has made every attempt to contact the copyright holder. If anyone has any information please contact licensing@brownbearbooks.co.uk

Manufactured in the United States of America

CPSIA compliance information: Batch #CW15GS. For further information contact Gareth Stevens, New York, New York at 1-800-542-2595.

CONTENTS

AT ODDS

HAMILTON Vs. BURR

Founding Father Alexander Hamilton (1757–1804) was a talented and charming character who divided loyalties and caused controversy throughout his life.

* Hamilton was the illegimate son of unmarried parents who both died when their son was still very young.

* Hamilton was born on St. Croix in the West Indies.

* Local landowners paid for Hamilton to attend Columbia College, New York.

* He became a general in the Revolutionary War (1775–1783) and secretary of the treasury from 1789 to 1795.

Despite being unpopular with many contemporaries, Aaron Burr (1756–1836) inspired great loyalty in others. Having become a successful attorney he turned his attention to politics. He rose to the second highest office in the country, vice president.

* Burr was born into a prominent and privileged New Jersey family, but was orphaned by the age of 2.

* He rose to the rank of colonel in the Revolutionary War.

* He attended Princeton University and qualified as a lawyer.

* Burr served as the third vice president of the United States of America from 1800 to 1804.

* Burr's letters filled just two volumes when they were collected; Hamilton's filled 27 books.

CONTEXT

The Revolutionary War (1775–1783) ended when the British army commanded by Charles Cornwallis surrendered at Yorktown, Virginia, on October 19, 1781. The victory confirmed the independence declared by the United States 5 years earlier.

The men who had led the Revolution now faced the challenge of creating a new country. At the time of the Declaration of Independence in July 1776, however, American victory was far from inevitable. When independence eventually came, many questions about the political shape of the new country still had to be decided.

General George Washington, the American commander in chief, kept his Continental Army together after the end of the war. During 1782

SURRENDER: The British surrender to American troops (right) and their French allies (left) at Yorktown in 1781.

COMMANDER: George Washington led the fight for American independence.

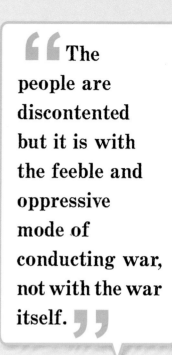

" The people are discontented but it is with the feeble and oppressive mode of conducting war, not with the war itself. **"**

George Washington, 1781

and 1783, he moved his army back to New York City to contain the British troops and oversee their departure. Peace between America and Britain was finally negotiated in Paris in 1783.

National Laws

To begin with, the new United States continued to use the laws that had been drafted during the war, the Articles of Confederation. The articles had been written intentionally so that they would be different from the laws the British had imposed on the American colonies.

One result of keeping the old Articles was that the new national government was weak. It had no powers to raise taxes, so it could

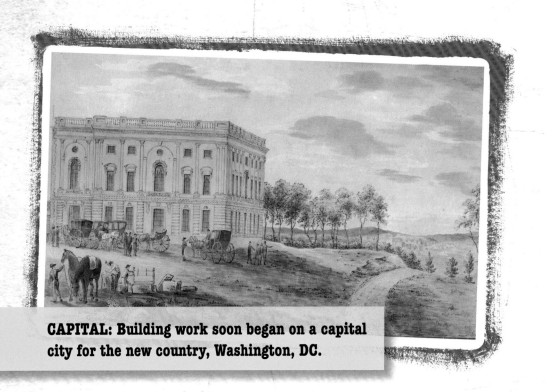

CAPITAL: Building work soon began on a capital city for the new country, Washington, DC.

not pay the soldiers of the Continental Army or the debts it owed foreign nations, such as France, who had helped pay for the war. It could also not afford to create a new national navy.

The Founders Disagree

It was clear that the country needed a new set of laws, but the Founding Fathers disagreed on what shape they should take. One group of people, known as the Federalists, wanted a strong, centralized national government. They included the former Continental Army commander Alexander Hamilton. The Federalists were opposed by a group known as the Republicans. The Republicans distrusted the idea of a central, federal government. They wanted more power to lie with the individual states, which were based upon the former colonies. The Republican group included the former army commander Aaron Burr, along with Thomas Jefferson, drafter of the Declaration of Independence.

A New Constitution

In the summer of 1787, each state sent delegates to Philadelphia to work out a new set of laws. George Washington was one of the delegates. The Federalist delegate James Madison arrived with a proposal he had written with the help of Alexander Hamilton. Although the delegates argued fiercely over points such as how to divide the two houses of Congress, Madison's Virginia Plan would form the basis of the new US Constitution.

President Washington

The one point all the delegates agreed on was who should be the first president of the United States of America. George Washington was the unanimous choice. He became president in 1789.

CAPITOL: The Founding Fathers discussed the best form of government.

" I believe the British government forms the best model the world ever produced. "

Alexander Hamilton, 1787

ALEXANDER HAMILTON

With his unusual background, Hamilton was to have a lasting effect on the economic development of young America.

Alexander Hamilton was born in the West Indies in around 1757. He was the illegitimate son of a Scottish nobleman and a French woman. Orphaned at an early age, the young man was sent by local businessmen to be educated in North America in 1772. Hamilton studied in New York, but was eager to join the growing revolutionary movement against British rule. He joined a militia unit and later became aide-de-camp to George Washington because of his ability to write and speak fluent French.

Despite fighting for the American cause, Hamilton was a strong supporter of Britain's monarchy. He wanted the United States to model its own government on that of Britain.

CHARMER: Hamilton's charm and talent helped his rise in US society.

WAR: Hamilton came to Washington's notice during the Revolutionary War.

Political Service

In 1789, Hamilton served as secretary of the treasury in Washington's first cabinet. Hamilton had a better understanding of financial matters than any of the other Founding Fathers. He wanted an economy based on investment, industry, and expanded commerce—and without slavery. Hamilton set up the government-owned Bank of the United States. He also organized debt repayments by bringing the financial debts of each state under the control of the federal goverment.

" There are few men to be found, of his age, who has a more general knowledge than he possesses, and none whose Soul is more firmly engaged in the cause. "

George Washington on Hamilton, 1781

AARON BURR

Burr is now best remembered as the man who killed Alexander Hamilton, but he had notable achievements to his name.

Aaron Burr was born into one of the oldest families of New Jersey, but was orphaned by the age of 2. He later excelled at Princeton before joining the Continental Army. At the end of the Revolutionary War, he practiced as a lawyer, first in Albany, New York, and then in New York City, where he moved in 1783.

BURR: This portrait shows Burr later in his life, long after the infamous duel.

A Political Career

After a successful legal career, Burr entered politics as a New York assemblyman in 1784, serving for a term. In 1789, the governor of New York appointed Burr as the state's attorney general. Burr also served as a senator for New York from 1791 to 1797.

Burr was very effective at rallying support from voters. He worked closely with local social clubs and groups. Some people believe he was in this way the first modern political campaigner.

FAMILY: After his wife's death in 1794, Burr became very close to his daughter, Theodosia.

Siding with the States

Like Thomas Jefferson, the secretary of state, Burr believed that each state should control its own affairs. Burr's support for Jefferson led to his highest political appointment. When Jefferson became president, Burr served as vice president from 1800 to 1804. After the duel with Hamilton, however, Burr's political career was dead. He fled to the West to try his political ambitions there.

> **" I never thought him an honest, frank-dealing man, but considered him as a crooked gun, or other perverted machine, whose aim or stroke you could never be sure of. "**

Thomas Jefferson on Burr, 1780s

POLITICAL CONTACTS

» FRIENDS AND ENEMIES

Popular and charismatic, Alexander Hamilton was able to count President George Washington among his many influential friends.

Throughout his life, Hamilton's obvious abilities made it easy for him to attract the friendship of important people. Having served with George Washington during the Revolutionary War, Hamilton remained close to him. He even helped Washington to write his farewell address when Washington left the presidency in March 1797.

JAY: Chief Justice John Jay supported Hamilton's opposition to slavery.

ENEMY: Thomas Jefferson was Hamilton's constant opponent.

Chief Justice

Many of Hamilton's friends were fellow Federalists such as James Madison and John Jay, the first chief justice of the US Supreme Court. Both Jay and Hamilton opposed slavery, and as governor of New York State, Jay introduced a law in 1799 to free slaves in the state.

Thomas Jefferson

Hamilton had the ability to work with people even when he did not agree with them. He and Thomas Jefferson had very different views about how the United States should develop. But Hamilton supported Jefferson over fellow Federalist John Adams in the 1800 presidential election. He believed that Jefferson would be better for the future of the country.

" Hamilton is really a colossus to the anti-republican party. Without numbers, he is an host within himself. "

Thomas Jefferson, 1782

COMPLEX LOYALTIES

Many people were suspicious of Aaron Burr and his political motives, but he inspired great devotion from his family and his close friends.

Burr divided opinion among the other Founding Fathers, and he was also capable of changing his own attitudes toward his friends. In 1797, Burr was friendly enough with James Monroe, who later became the fifth president of the United States, to act as Monroe's second, or supporter in a duel. But in 1815, Burr wrote a letter saying that his former friend was "below mediocrity."

MONROE: Burr fell out with his former friend, James Monroe.

66 His generalship, perseverance, industry, and execution exceeds all description, so that I think I can say he deserves anything and everything of his country. 99

James Nicholson on Burr, 1800

SECOND: William Van Ness was Burr's second at the duel with Hamilton.

Close Friends

Burr did have close friends, however. They included John Adams and Andrew Jackson—the second and seventh presidents, respectively—and chief justice and New York governor John Jay, who was also a friend of Hamilton. Burr was generous to his friends and gave away much of the money he earned from his legal practice. Lawyer William Van Ness accompanied Burr as his second to the duel with Hamilton and later wrote a pamphlet defending Burr's conduct.

Loving Family

Burr's closest companions were his family. His devoted wife, Theodosia Bartow Prevost, died very young in 1794, robbing him of his closest companion. Burr then became very close to his daughter, also called Theodosia, who was born in 1783. He was determined that Theodosia should have the same educational opportunities as a boy of her age. He was heartbroken when she drowned in 1813.

LINES ARE DRAWN

The political divisions between Hamilton and Burr first became apparent in the first discussions about the new US Constitution.

When delegates from the states met in Philadelphia in 1787 to discuss a new set of laws by which the United States would be governed, it was soon clear that there would be no broad agreement. The delegates split into two groups. One group, who became known as the Federalists, wanted power to lie in the hands of a central government that would govern all 13 existing states and any new states that might be created. The other group—known as the Republicans or the Democratic-Republicans—believed each state should be able to control its own affairs.

CONVENTION: The convention met in Philadelphia to draft a new constitution.

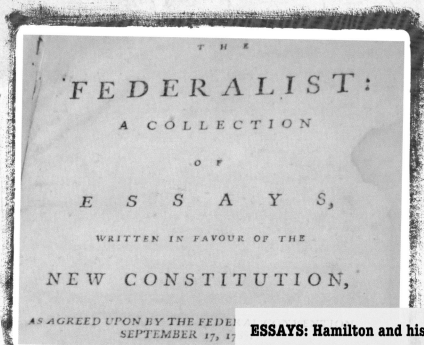

ESSAYS: Hamilton and his friends wrote at length about writing the new constitution.

Opposite Sides

Alexander Hamilton and Aaron Burr had both served with George Washington during the Revolutionary War. They had become friends, although Burr was never as close to Washington as Hamilton. In the debates about the Constitution, however, they had found themselves to be on different sides. Hamilton was a confirmed Federalist. Burr, meanwhile, had less fixed political ideas, although he was a supporter of Thomas Jefferson, who was one of the leaders of the Republicans.

> **Burr's integrity as an individual is not unimpeached. As a public man he is one of the worst sort: a friend to nothing but as it suits his interest and ambition.**

Alexander Hamilton, 1782

Putting His Case

Aaron Burr had been suggested as a delegate to the Constitutional Convention, but he did not attend. Hamilton did go, however, as a representative for New York. The other delegates thought Hamilton was too radical. He suggested that both the president and senators should be elected for life. Hamilton did not get his way on this, but he still signed the Constitution on September 17, 1787.

The US Constitution was more Federalist than Democratic—Republicans had wanted. With his friends John Jay and James Madison, Hamilton published a series of essays known as *The Federalist Papers* to promote it. The 85 essays were published under the mysterious name "Publius."

SIGNATURE: Hamilton was the only New York delegate to sign the US Constitution.

A Two-Party System

The origin of America's modern two-party system dates back to the divisions that first opened between the Founding Fathers at the Constitutional Convention. The Federalists and the Democratic-Republicans soon emerged as the first political parties. The Democratic-Republicans usually became known more simply just as the Republican Party.

ADDRESS
OF THE LATE
GENERAL GEORGE WASHINGTON.
To the Citizens of the United States, on declining a re-election to the Office of President.

FAREWELL: Hamilton helped Washington write his farewell address as president.

> **He is unprincipled, both as a public and private man. He is determined to make his way to the head of the popular party.**

Hamilton on Burr, 1792

Hamilton and Burr were on different sides of the constitutional debates. Hamilton was a leader of the Federalists, while Burr was a supporter of the Republican Thomas Jefferson. Still, the two men managed to remain on friendly terms. The split between them was about to widen, however, and this time the cause was not entirely political. It would have a personal aspect that would change the lives of both men.

HOSTILITIES BEGIN

The first real clash between Hamilton and Burr came in 1791, when Hamilton's father-in-law ran for election to the US Senate.

In December 1780, Alexander Hamilton married Elizabeth Schuyler, the daughter of the New York landowner and Revolutionary general Philip Schuyler. Many observers thought the marriage marked Hamilton's arrival at the very peak of US society, although others believed that it was Philip Schuyler who was lucky to have acquired such a talented son-in-law who was clearly destined for great things.

Philip Schuyler was a Federalist who counted George Washington, John Adams, and Hamilton among his friends and political allies. He had been elected to the Senate for New York when the first senatorial elections were held in 1789. At the time, the electoral process was complex, and states could decide how often to elect their senators. New York had decided its senators would serve for only 2 years, so Schuyler was up for reelection in 1791.

SCHUYLER: Philip Schuyler was from one of New York's leading families.

FRANCE: The Republicans supported the aims of the French Revolution but not its violent methods.

A Complicated System

Although Schuyler still lived in his hometown, Albany, in upstate New York, his main support came from around New York City. The state's political makeup was not straightforward, however. Alexander Hamilton had been the only one of its representatives to sign the new US Constitution. Others opposed a federal government, which they thought would produce a political aristocracy like the British rulers the Americans had just fought against. The Republicans, meanwhile, supported the overthrow of monarchy, such as the rebellion that began in France in 1789.

> **If you have the same Opinion of Mr Burr that many have, you will not rely much on his friendship.**
>
> Morgan Lewis, 1791

> **"** Give me the Sum Of thousand dollars and I will leve the town. **"**

James Reynolds, blackmail letter to Hamilton, 1791

SCANDAL: Hamilton's wife, Elizabeth, stood by him during the scandal.

Vote for Burr!

Aaron Burr had been careful to remain on good terms with both the Federalists and the Republicans in New York State. But when the Republicans asked him to become their candidate for senator, he agreed. He had worked as a lawyer in New York City and was well known there. That helped him to win enough votes to defeat Schuyler in 1791 and take his seat in the US Senate (although he would lose it again in 1796).

For Hamilton, the senatorial election marked a decisive change in his friendship with Burr. They had managed to stay on reasonably friendly terms despite their political differences. But in Hamilton's eyes, Burr had now insulted his father-in-law and, by extension, himself by agreeing to stand as a Republican against Schuyler. From now on, some of the opinions Hamilton expressed about his former friend would become far more hostile. For his part, however, Burr kept his opinions to himself. It was a notable aspect of his character that Burr was rarely critical of others.

A Partisan Scandal

Meanwhile, Hamilton's political views became mixed up with his personal life. In 1791, Hamilton began a relationship with a woman named Maria Reynolds. Her husband, James Reynolds, blackmailed Hamilton to try to keep the affair secret. When the news finally became public, more rumors began about Hamilton's private life. Some of the rumors were started by his political opponent, the Republican Thomas Jefferson. The scandal ended Hamilton's political career. He resigned as Secretary of the Treasury in 1795 and never held public office again. When Maria Reynolds divorced her husband in 1797, the attorney she enlisted was none other than Aaron Burr.

A Falling Out

Meanwhile, Hamilton had also fallen out with his Federalist colleague, John Adams, who became president in 1797. French vessels began seizing American ships as part of the so-called Quasi War, a conflict that took place from 1798 to 1800, based largely on a historic rivalry between France and Britain. Hamilton believed Adams' response to the French actions was too weak. This would have serious consequences on the election of 1800.

ENEMY: Although John Adams and Hamilton were both Federalists, they hated each other.

ELECTION OF 1800

The dislike between Alexander Hamilton and Aaron Burr flared up again during the presidential election of 1800.

After serving two terms as president of the United States, George Washington stood down in 1796. His successor was the man who had served as vice president in both terms, the Federalist John Adams. Whereas Washington's original election had been unanimous, Adams's election in 1796 was notable for the mudslinging that took place. The 1800 election was even worse.

ADAMS: This poster supported Adams' second campaign for president.

BAYARD: James Bayard led the Federalist campaign against Burr in the House of Representatives.

> " It was to be expected that the enemy would endeavor to sow weeds between us, that they might divide us and our friends. "
>
> **Jefferson writes to Burr, 1801**

Party Divisions

In the 1800 election, Adams stood for a second term against his previous opponent, the Republican Thomas Jefferson. During John Adams' first administration, he had faced fierce opposition not only from Jefferson and the Republicans, but also from a wing of the Federalists led by his hated rival, Alexander Hamilton.

In the first election, Adams had defeated Jefferson by just three

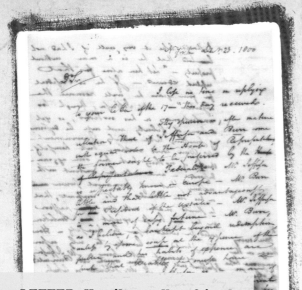

LETTER: Hamilton tells a friend why he is supporting Jefferson.

votes in the electoral college. This time, whoever took New York would take the presidency—and Aaron Burr was the key to the Democratic–Republican vote in New York.

Plotting for Power

Although Hamilton thought Adams was a poor president, he also disliked Jefferson. He did not oppose Adams openly, which would hand the presidency to Jefferson. Instead, he endorsed the Federalist candidate for vice president, Charles Cotesworth Pinckney, as president. Meanwhile, Jefferson supported Burr for the vice presidency, which he hoped would secure the New York vote.

In order to run for the vice presidency, a candidate had to run for the presidency but come second. Each member of the electoral college had two votes for president. To make sure one candidate from their favored party got more votes and became president, one elector had to withhold his vote from the other candidate, who would come second and become vice president.

> " I will never more be responsible for Adams by my direct support, even though the consequence should be the election of Jefferson. "
>
> **Alexander Hamilton, May 1800**

ELECTED: Thomas Jefferson was president from 1801 until 1809.

The Election

The 1800 election took place from April to October. New York was the first state to vote, and Burr's presence on the ticket helped the Democratic-Republicans win. The pattern was repeated throughout the country. By the end of the voting, the Republicans were ahead by eight electoral college votes. The Republicans had clearly won, but none of the Republican electors remembered to withhold their vote. The result was that Burr and Jefferson tied for the presidency. The House of Representatives had to decide the president.

Hamilton, as leader of the Federalists, decided to support his enemy Jefferson over his enemy Burr. After a series of 36 ballots that went on until February 1801, Jefferson was elected as third president of the United States. Burr was furious with Hamilton's decision, and the hatred between the two men grew deeper.

COOPER'S LETTER

It was only when a letter appeared in the *Albany Register* that Burr came to understand how much Hamilton seemed to hate him.

On April 12, 1804, Dr. Charles D. Cooper of Albany wrote a private letter in which he discussed comments that Hamilton had made about Burr at a dinner at which he, Cooper, had been present. Hamilton had called his old friend "despicable," a strong insult. The letter ended up being published in the Republican newspaper, the *Albany Register*, which also printed more letters between Cooper and Philip Schuyler. In one letter, Cooper suggested that Hamilton had said worse things about Burr than those that had been reported.

ALBANY: Cooper's letter was published in the Republican newspaper in Albany.

Njork 13 June 1804

Sir

I send for your perusal a letter signed Ch. D. Cooper which though apparently published some time ago, has but very recently come to my knowledge.— Mr. Van Ness who does me the favor to deliver this, will point out to you that clause of the letter to which I particularly request your attention.

You must perceive, Sir, the necessity of a prompt and unqualified acknowledgment or denial of the use of any expressions which could warrant the assertions of Dr. Cooper.

I have the honor to be
your ob'l'st.
A. Burr

Genl Hamilton

> **RESPONSE:** When Burr heard about the story, he at once wrote asking Hamilton to explain himself.

Burr's Response

Burr learned of Hamilton's alleged comments on June 18, 1804. He wrote to Hamilton to try to get to the bottom of what had been said. If Hamilton had made rude comments about Burr, Burr wanted an apology. However, Hamilton refused to apologize. Instead, he wrote a vague response that did not appear to take Burr's letter seriously. The enraged Burr challenged Hamilton to a duel.

> " **Although apparently published some time ago, this has but recently come to my knowledge.** "

Burr writes to Hamilton, June 18, 1804.

THE DUEL

Both men initially thought a duel could be avoided, but it soon became clear that the confrontation would take place.

Burr had written to Hamilton seeking an apology for the slander reported in Cooper's letter. When Hamilton did not apologize, Burr challenged Hamilton to a duel, which Hamilton accepted.

At the time, dueling remained an accepted way for gentlemen to settle disputes about their honor, although it was illegal in New York and would shortly be outlawed across the North. A whole code had

LOCATION: Weehawken was popular for duels because it was outside New York, where dueling was forbidden.

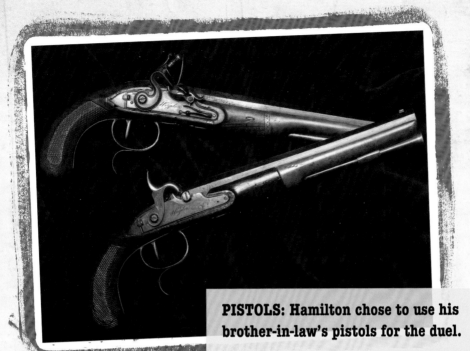

PISTOLS: Hamilton chose to use his brother-in-law's pistols for the duel.

grown up about the staging of a duel and how both men should behave. Most duels were not fatal. In many, both participants shot wide of their target, which allowed them both to preserve their honor. Both Hamilton and Burr had fought duels before. Hamilton's eldest son, Philip, had been killed in a duel just 3 years earlier.

Countdown to Death

The duel was arranged for July 11, 1804, at Weehawken in New Jersey. Both men went about their business as normal until the night before the duel, when they both wrote letters setting out what they wanted to happen if they were killed. In his letter, Alexander Hamilton

> " Pendleton knows I did not mean to fire at Colonel Burr the first time. "
>
> Hamilton, July 11, 1804.

> ## "This is a mortal wound, Doctor."

Alexander Hamilton, July 11, 1804

claimed he was against dueling and said that he would deliberately miss Burr with his shot. Aaron Burr's letter was mainly about his wishes for the continuing education of his daughter, Theodosia.

The Duel

At dawn on July 11, 1804, the two men and their seconds were rowed separately from Manhattan across the Hudson River to Weehawken. William Van Ness was Burr's second, while Hamilton's second was Judge Nathaniel Pendleton. They were accompanied by a doctor named David Hosack, who would provide medical assistance.

The site of the duel was a narrow ledge at the foot of a cliff. It was surrounded by trees and was a popular site for duels because it was isolated. Hamilton brought a pair of ornate dueling pistols belonging

DUEL: This drawing of the duel is from the artist's imagination. No one witnessed the actual shooting.

UPON THIS STONE RESTED
THE HEAD OF THE PATRIOT
SOLDIER, STATESMAN, AND
JURIST ALEXANDER HAMILTON,
AFTER THE DUEL WITH
AARON BURR.

ROCK: This memorial stone marks the site of the duel in Weehawken.

to his brother-in-law to use as weapons. He chose to fire from the end of the ledge that looked into the rising sun.

Starting back to back, the two men walked 10 paces away from each other and then loaded their pistols. Once they were in position, each man could fire as he wanted. Two shots rang out. Hamilton's shot missed Burr and hit a tree branch, but Burr's shot hit Hamilton above his hips. Who fired first is not clear; neither is it clear whether Hamilton missed deliberately or whether Burr meant to hit Hamilton. The seconds did not actually watch the duel in order to avoid being implicated in an illegal activity.

What was soon clear, however, was that Hamilton's wound was fatal. He was rowed back across the Hudson River to New York and survived until the next day, when he died from the wound at a friend's house where he had been taken.

A MARTYR'S DEATH

Public grief and shock greeted the news of Hamilton's death. New Yorkers saw the dead man as a modern-day martyr.

New York was gripped by news of Hamilton's death at the age of 49. Newspapers described the duel in detail, even though the actual shooting was shrouded in mystery because no one had seen it. Everyone wanted to know whether Hamilton had fired first or not. Many people saw Vice President Burr as a murderer who was determined to kill Hamilton. In contrast, newspapers compared Hamilton with great heroes of the ancient world like Alexander the Great and hailed him as the "son of Washington." In private, however,

REPORT: Hamilton's funeral was reported in the New York papers.

MONUMENT: Hamilton's tomb was based on the design of an Egyptian pyramid.

some of his political colleagues were not so generous. They criticized his complicated personal life and his political maneuvering.

The Funeral

Hamilton's funeral was held 2 days after he died. There had been nothing like it since the funeral of George Washington 5 years earlier.

Hamilton's gray horse followed his mahogany coffin, carrying his boots and spurs reversed in the stirrups. Hamilton's widow, Elizabeth, and seven surviving children were followed in the parade by the political and legal leaders of New York, public figures, and hundreds of New Yorkers who paid tribute to the dead man.

> **Newspapers will announce and explain to you the public misfortune experienced here by the untimely death of Hamilton.**

George Cabot writes from New York to a friend in Boston, July 18, 1804

BURR'S CONSPIRACY

» A CONTROVERSIAL ADVENTURE

Burr was taken aback by the public outpouring of grief that greeted Hamilton's death. He soon realized his political career was over.

In death, Hamilton had succeeded doing what he had failed to accomplish while he lived: he had ruined the career of Burr. Burr initially fled to South Carolina but later returned north to serve out his remaining term as vice president, even though he was indicted for murder. When Burr ran in the 1804 election for governor of New York, he lost by 9,000 votes, the heaviest defeat then known. Many New Yorkers blamed him for Hamilton's death. Burr's political aspirations were a thing of the past.

REVOLT: Burr was accused of trying to raise an army to seize Mexico.

CAPTURE: Burr flees after the failure of his apparent plot against the United States.

Treason?

Although Burr was indicted for Hamilton's murder, he was never brought to trial. In 1805, he headed west into Louisiana Territory, which President Jefferson had just bought from France. Burr was accused of trying to provoke a rebellion in Louisiana in order to unite Louisiana with Mexico and proclaim himself emperor. Burr was arrested and tried for treason, but eventually acquitted of all charges.

In 1808, Burr went to Europe. He returned to New York in 1812, and lived there quietly but in relative poverty until his death in 1836, aged 80.

> " Oh Burr, oh Burr, what hast thou done? Thou hast shooted dead great Hamilton! You hid behind a bunch of thistle, And shooted him dead with a great hoss pistol! "

Verse pinned to Burr's door, 1804

AFTERMATH

History has not judged Aaron Burr well, but Alexander Hamilton continues to be revered as one of the nation's Founding Fathers.

Aaron Burr's death in 1836 attracted little attention compared with the nation's deep mourning for Hamilton over 30 years earlier. Unlike Hamilton, Burr was born with every advantage but made little of himself. His political career—even though he became vice president—is seen as a result of the political system rather than personal popularity, although Burr is often credited with being the first modern political campaigner. Burr did not look for favor and rarely cared what people thought of him. At the end of his life, Burr admitted that he should not have challenged Hamilton to the duel but should, instead, have learned to accept Hamilton's criticisms.

STATUE: Hamilton's statue stands outside the US Treasury Building in Washington, DC.

NOTES: Hamilton's face is still featured on US $10 bills.

Founding Father

Hamilton's legacy has been greater than Burr's. His many personal failings are often forgotten, particularly as his early death helped make him an idealized figure. For many people, his story remains a great example of the American dream. He showed that character and hard work could take anyone to the top of their profession.

Hamilton is credited with the forward-looking economic vision that helped to establish the financial system on which the United States is still based. The country today is largely as Hamilton imagined it: an urban manufacturing center that attracts people and business from all over the world.

> **I should have known that the world was wide enough for Hamilton and me.**

Aaron Burr, late in his life

JUDGMENT

HAMILTON Vs. BURR

The intense rivalry between Hamilton and Burr ended with Hamilton's death. But whose reputation would endure more strongly over time?

* Hamilton is still revered as one of the Founding Fathers, but even some of his allies were critical of some of his behavior.

* Hamilton's role in building the new American nation has outweighed his faults.

* Hamilton's relationship with Maria Reynolds caused a scandal and all but ended his career.

* Hamilton's biggest legacy, the shaping of the American economy, was not universally approved of at the time.

Aaron Burr was condemned as a murderer, even though his actions during the duel were within the dueling code. His later actions in Louisiana were even more controversial.

* Unlike Hamilton, Burr's political accomplishments were relatively modest and are rarely remembered.

* Despite Burr's poor reputation, he did not create scandal like Hamilton did.

* Burr was accused of treason for his "conspiracy" in the Louisiana Territory, but was acquitted of the charges at his trial.

* Burr did not express any strong regret for his role in the death of Hamilton.

* Unlike Hamilton, Burr rarely expressed negative opinions about his contemporaries.

TIMELINE

Although the rivalry between Hamilton and Burr came to a dramatic head in 1804, the political and personal differences between them had developed over the course of at least a decade.

A New King
Former Revolutionary War colonel and New York lawyer Aaron Burr is elected to a seat in the New York State Assembly.

Federal Papers
Hamilton and his fellow Federalists, James Madison and John Jay, write a long series of essays known as the *Federal Papers* in support of the new constitution.

A Personal Slight
Hamilton takes personal offense when his father-in-law, Philip Schuyler, is defeated by Burr in the election for New York senator.

1784   **1787**   **1789**   **1791**   **1797**

New Taxes
In May, Hamilton attends the Constitutional Convention, which sees arguments between the Federalists and the Democratic-Republicans.

Treasury Secretary
Alexander Hamilton becomes secretary of the treasury under George Washington; he creates a national bank and a federal economic system.

Hamilton's Scandal
Hamilton's career in public office is ended when he is forced to reveal details of his affair with a married woman, Maria Reynolds.

Unauthorized Publication
In October, Burr publishes private criticisms Hamilton has made of President John Adams, which Hamilton had never intended to be made public.

Divisive Election Highest Office
In March, Burr achieves his highest political office when he becomes vice president to President Thomas Jefferson.

Cooper's Letter
In April, the *Albany Register* publishes a letter from Dr. Charles Cooper that reports negative comments made by Hamilton about Burr. Hamilton refuses Burr's request to apologize.

1800 **1801**   **1804**

Divisive Election
In February, Hamilton decides not to give the backing of the Federalists to Burr in the tied presidential election with Thomas Jefferson. Jefferson becomes president.

Another Election
In February, Hamilton campaigns against Burr's election as governor of New York. Burr loses by a landslide to the Republican Morgan Lewis.

Fatal Duel
In July, Burr and Hamilton duel over Hamilton's comments about Burr. Hamilton's shot misses, but he is mortally wounded and dies the next day.

GLOSSARY

acquit To find someone not guilty in a criminal trial.

affair A secret relationship involving at least one married person.

aide-de-camp A military officer who serves as an assistant to a senior commander.

Articles of Confederation The laws drawn up for the government of the thirteen colonies during the Revolutionary War.

blackmail To illegally demand money in order to keep something secret.

duel An arranged contest with deadly weapons between two people to settle a point of honor.

federal A form of government in which individual states are subject to a central national government.

Federalist A supporter of the Federalist Party, which backed the creation of a strong national government.

illegitimate Describes a child born to unmarried parents.

indict To formally charge someone with committing a crime.

martyr A person who chooses to die to support his or her cause or beliefs.

mudslinging The use of unjustified or unsupported insults and accusations to damage the reputation of an opponent.

pamphlet A small, thin book with a paper cover.

partisan Strongly connected with a particular political party or cause.

Republican A supporter of the Democratic-Republican Party, which wanted to leave political power with the individual states.

second Someone who assists a participant in a duel.

slander The act of saying something false that damages a person's reputation.

treason The act of planning to overthrow the government of your own country.

untimely Before the natural or proper time.

FOR FURTHER INFORMATION

Books

Burgan, Michael. *Soldier and Founder: Alexander Hamilton* (We the People: Revolution and the New Nation). We the People, 2009.

Dunn, John M. *The Constitution and Founding of America* (American History). Lucent Books, 2007.

Gould, Jane H. *Alexander Hamilton* (Jr. Graphic Founding Fathers). PowerKids Press, 2012.

Greeley, August. *Pistols and Politics: Alexander Hamilton's Great Duel* (Great Moments in American History). Rosen Publishing Group, 2004.

Melton, Buckner F., Jr. *Aaron Burr: The Rise and Fall of an American Politician* (Library of American Lives and Times). PowerKids Press, 2003.

Roberts, Russell. *Alexander Hamilton* (Profiles in American History). Mitchell Lane Publishers, 2006.

Websites

http://www.pbs.org/wgbh/amex/duel
Extensive website to support the PBS documentary *The Duel*.

http://www.history.com/topics/american-revolution/alexander-hamilton
History.com page with videos about Hamilton and the Founding Fathers.

http://www.biography.com/people/alexander-hamilton-9326481
Biography.com page on Hamilton, with a video biography.

http://www.biography.com/people/aaron-burr-9232241
Biography.com pages on Aaron Burr's life, including his career after the duel.

Publisher's note to educators and parents: Our editors have carefully reviewed these websites to ensure that they are suitable for students. Many websites change frequently, however, and we cannot guarantee that a site's future contents will continue to meet our high standards of quality and educational value. Be advised that students should be closely supervised whenever they access the Internet.

INDEX